Handwriting

Resources
and Assessment

BOOK 3 AND BOOK 4

Anita Warwick

Series editor: John Jackman
Original authors: Louis Fidge and Peter Smith

Published in 2003 by:
Nelson Thornes Ltd
Delta Place
27 Bath Road
CHELTENHAM
GL53 7TH
United Kingdom

07 05 08 09 / 10 9 8 7 6 5 4

A catalogue record for this book is available from the British Library

ISBN 978 0 7487 7007 6

Illustrations by Mike Phillips
Cover illustration by Lisa Smith
Logo illustration by Woody Fox
Page make-up by Green House Design, Bookham, Surrey

Printed and bound in Croatia by Zrinski

Acknowledgements

Acknowledgement has been made to Alexander Inglis as the original developer of the Nelson
Handwriting script.

'Ballooning Over London', 'Fly a Flag', 'The Seedling', 'Alphabet Story', 'Buried Treasure', verse
from 'Poem Power', each © Ronald Kay 2003, reprinted by permission of the author; 'Rainy
Nights' by Irene Thompson from *The Book of a Thousand Poems* (Bell and Hyman, 1983);
'Fruit Salad' by Gina Douthwaite; lines about Nicholas Fisk, reprinted by permission of Penguin
Books Ltd; 'Seal' by William Jay Smith and 'Catalog' by Rosalie Moore from *The Golden
Treasury of Poetry*, selected by Louise Untermayer (Collins, 1961); 'A Blink' by Jacqueline
Segal; 'Humpty Dumpty Went to the Moon' © 1979 Michael Rosen from *A First Book of Poetry*
(OUP), reprinted by permission of PFD on behalf of the author; 'If Things Grew Down' by
Robert D. Hoeft; lines about 'The Mysterious Sphinx' from *The Encyclopedia of the Ancient
World* (Southwater Publishing, 2000); 'MissionEarth' © Clive Webster, reprinted by permission
of the author; extract about 'Seat Belts' from *The Highway Code* © Crown Copyright 1999;
'Astronauts and Crosses' by Paul Sidley; lines about 'Medusa' from *Ancient Greek Myths and
Legends* by Philip Ardagh (Belitha Press, 1997); 'Lost' by James Godden; lines from 'A Flight
to Italy' by D. Day Lewis from *The Complete Poems of C. Day Lewis* (Sinclair Stevenson, 1992).

Every effort has been made to trace the copyright holders, but if any have been inadvertently
overlooked the publishers will be pleased to make the necessary arrangements at the first
opportunity.

Nelson
Handwriting

Contents

How to use this book

The *Developing Skills* book provides the core handwriting curriculum for the year. It is differentiated to ensure children can progress through key stages in handwriting at their own pace.

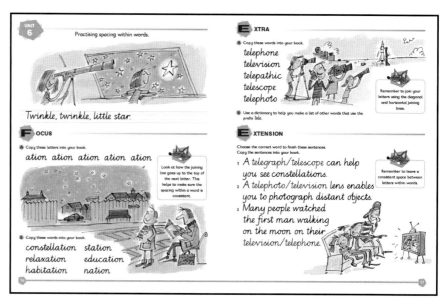

There are two copymasters in this book to go with each Unit in the *Developing Skills* book:

The **Focus Resource** is designed for the less-able pupil who needs further practice in the basic teaching point.

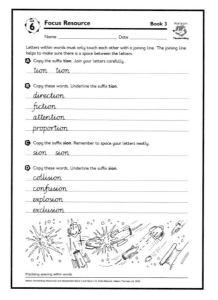

The **Extension Resource** caters for the child who needs more demanding work arising from, or linked to, the Unit teaching point.

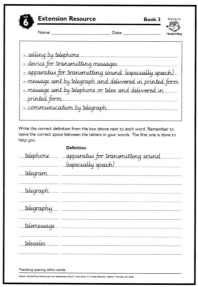

Nelson Handwriting Resources and Assessment Book 3 and Book 4 © Anita Warwick, Nelson Thornes Ltd, 2003

Assessment

This book also contains a range of easy-to-administer assessment sheets. These are designed to be used flexibly and come in three forms:

Placement Tests – these can be used at the start of the year to give an overview of a class's handwriting ability. The Tests can be checked against the **LevellingGuide** contained in this book.

The **Handwriting Assessment Record Sheet** is a quick and easy reference tool for the teacher to use to record the level of each child's handwriting.

Self-assessment Sheets – these reinforce the self-assessment aspect of Nelson Handwriting introduced in the *Workbooks*. The Sheets take pupils through aspects of their handwriting that they need to check. The aim is to help the process become automatic for pupils.

General Assessment Sheets – these are included for each of the main teaching focuses and can be used for extra practice or to check how pupils are coping with the different handwriting challenges.

Also included in this *Resources and Assessment* book are **Guidelines** of the appropriate width, and a helpful left-handed version of the **Getting Ready to Write** flap from the *Developing Skills* books to give to left-handed pupils.

Levelling Guide

For use with **Placement Tests**

These level descriptors should be used alongside the Placement tests in this book. Comparing your pupil's handwriting to the descriptors here will help you place the handwriting ability of your pupils and chart their progress. For more information see page 18 of the Teacher's Book.

England and Wales

Level 1   'Letters are usually clearly shaped and correctly oriented.'

Level 2   'In handwriting, letters are accurately formed and consistent in size.'

Level 3   'Handwriting is joined and legible.'

Level 4   'Handwriting style is fluent, joined and legible.'

Level 5   'Handwriting is joined clear and fluent and, where appropriate, is adapted to a range of tasks.'

Scotland

Level A   In writing tasks pupils 'form letters and space words legibly for the most part. At an appropriate stage, linkage of letters will be taught.'

Level B   In writing tasks pupils 'form letters and space words legibly in linked script'.

Level C   In writing tasks pupils 'employ a fluent, legible style of handwriting'.

Level D   In writing tasks pupils 'employ a fluent, legible style of handwriting and set out completed work giving attention to presentation and layout'.

Level E   In writing tasks pupils 'employ a fluent, legible style of handwriting, and set out completed work clearly and attractively'.

Northern Ireland

Level 1   'Pupils should show some control over the size, shape and orientation of letters.'

Level 2   'There is evidence of the use of upper and lower case letters.'

Level 3   'Handwriting is accurately formed and consistant in size.'

Level 4   'Handwriting is swift and legible.'

Level 5   'Handwriting is swift and legible.'

Nelson Handwriting Resources and Assessment Book 3 and Book 4 © Anita Warwick, Nelson Thornes Ltd, 2003

Getting ready to write

For use by left-handed pupils

Are you sitting comfortably with both feet on the floor?

Are you holding your pen correctly?

Is your paper at the correct angle?

Nelson
Handwriting

Handwriting Assessment Record Sheet 1

Child's name _____ Right or left-handed _____

Tick or date entries, making any comments as necessary.

Ready to write

Is the child ready to write? Does he/she:

- sit correctly (both feet on the floor, leaning forward, not too close to the table)?
- hold the pencil in an appropriate tripod grip?
- position the paper correctly?

Basic letter movements

Can he/she make the following patterns:
- swings?
- bridges?
- straight lines?
- diagonals?
- spirals?
- **c** pattern?

Construction of letters

Does he/she:

- make pencil strokes smoothly and without undue pressure?
- use the correct movements when writing letters (see individual checklist)?
- make all letters the correct shape?
- ensure all letters are the correct size and height?
- make the down strokes parallel?
- make exit flicks as appropriate?
- write and use the different forms of **s**?

Nelson Handwriting Resources and Assessment Book 3 and Book 4 © Anita Warwick, Nelson Thornes Ltd, 2003

Nelson

Handwriting

Handwriting Assessment Record Sheet 2

Child's name _____ Right or left-handed _____

Tick or date entries, making any comments as necessary.

The four handwriting joins

Can he/she make the following joins correctly and as one
continuous movement:

- the first join – diagonal joins to letters without ascenders? ☐ _____

- the second join – diagonal joins to letters with ascenders? ☐ _____

- the third join – horizontal joins to letters without
  ascenders? ☐ _____

- the fourth join – horizontal joins to letters with ascenders? ☐ _____

Can he/she:

- use the break letters appropriately and with regular
  spacing? ☐ _____

- form and join the letter **f** correctly? ☐ _____

- form and join to the letter **e** correctly? ☐ _____

Size and spacing

Is he/she consistent in:

- the size and proportion of letters? ☐ _____

- spacing between letters (letters do not touch)? ☐ _____

- spacing between words? ☐ _____

Presentation

Does he/she:

- use a clear, neat hand in finished, presented work? ☐ _____

- slope writing slightly to the right? ☐ _____

- write fluently and legibly? ☐ _____

- write with speed, e.g. note-taking, lists? ☐ _____

- use informal writing for rough drafting? ☐ _____

- use a range of presentational skills, including: ☐ _____

  - print script for captions, sub headings and labels? ☐ _____

  - decorated borders (as appropriate)? ☐ _____

Nelson Handwriting Resources and Assessment Book 3 and Book 4 © Anita Warwick, Nelson Thornes Ltd, 2003   9

Nelson
Handwriting

Placement Test

Book 3 Level

Name _____   Date _____

The four handwriting joins

Can you make the joins correctly? Write these letters.

The first join

ad   ce   cc   do   dy

ha   ki   lm   tu   uv

The second join

ab   ef   il   ik   ut

sh   nl   cl   ll   uk

The third join

fo   fa   og   om   rp

ve   rd   rn   wo   wi

The fourth join

ff   fl   ol   oh   rt

rf   rl   rb   wl   wk

The break letters

be   go   ju   pi   qu

xa   ye   zo   bb   gg

Are each of the joins formed correctly? ☐

Are letters the correct size and height? ☐

Nelson Handwriting Resources and Assessment Book 3 and Book 4 © Anita Warwick, Nelson Thornes Ltd, 2003

Name _____   Date _____

Write this poem on to plain paper.

I'm Mister Shakespeare.
I pace the stage.
I'm one of the greatest
hits of the age.

My number ones
Are 'Hamlet' and 'Macbeth'.
I like to write
about blood and death.

Murderers lurking,
armies crashing –
stabbing, hacking,
skewering, slashing!

Axe and dagger,
pike and claymore –
this is what
the public pay for!

They're also fond
of booing and hissing
and they like a bit
of slobbery kissing!

From *'Mr Shakespeare'* by *Charles Thomson*

Is the handwriting joined and legible?   ☐
Is the handwriting fluent?   ☐
Is the poem set out neatly on the page?   ☐

Sloped writing

These things happened to Shireen last week. Decide on which day each thing happened and fill in Shireen's diary. Remember to slope your writing.

- I made friends with Nadine again.
- Uncle Saheed came to see me.
- I stayed up late to watch a film on T.V.
- I got all my spellings right.
- Mum took me shopping in town.
- We had art all afternoon.
- I was invited to Ben's party.

Diary of a good week

Sunday _____

_____

Monday _____

_____

Tuesday _____

_____

Wednesday _____

_____

Thursday _____

_____

Friday _____

_____

Saturday _____

_____

Are the letters formed correctly? ☐

Are letters the correct size and height? ☐

Is the spacing between letters and between words consistent? ☐

Name _____ Date _____

Punctuation

Write these sentences. Put in the missing capital letters and punctuation marks.

i think reading is my favourite hobby

what kind of book do you like best

i am very keen on books about sport

is that annas computer asked james

no said anwar its mine

our class enjoys a game of rounders

oh dear cried mrs brown i cant find our cat

Are the capital letters the same height as ascenders? ☐

Are the inverted commas the same height as ascenders? ☐

Is the writing neat, fluent and legible? ☐

Nelson

Handwriting

General Assessment

Book 3 Level

Name _____   Date _____

Printing

A Write this menu in the space below. Use print letters.

Menu

First course: Soup of the day

     or   Prawn cocktail

Second course: Chicken and chips

     or   Cheese and tomato pizza

Third course: Ice cream sundae

     or   Apple pie and custard

_____

_____

_____

_____

_____

_____

_____

_____

_____

B What would you choose from the menu? Print your choices here.

First course: _____

Second course: _____

Third course: _____

Are the letters clear and not joined?   ☐

Is the use of the print alphabet consistent?   ☐

Name _____   Date _____

Writing a playscript

This is the beginning of a story.

A Pop Group is Born

"Why don't we form a pop group?" said Emma.

"What shall we call ourselves?" asked Lisa.

"What about 'The Three Tops?'" said Lynsey.

"Where can we practise?" demanded Lisa.

"We could use our empty garage," said Lynsey.

"My brother has an electric guitar!" cried Emma

A Write the story as a playscript.

EMMA : Why don't we form a pop group?

LISA :

LYNSEY:

LISA :

LYNSEY:

EMMA :

B Now continue the play in your own words on a sheet of paper.

Is the play set out correctly? ☐

General Assessment

Book 3 Level

Name _____   Date _____

Drafting and editing

When we start to write a story we need to put our ideas down as quickly as we can, without worrying too much about our handwriting, spelling and punctuation. This is called drafting. It is one of the five steps in writing a story:

1. Plan the story – beginning, middle and end.
2. Draft the story.
3. Edit and improve the draft.
4. Check spelling, grammar and punctuation.
5. Write a neat, carefully written finished copy.

A HOLIDAY ADVENTURE

Last Orgust we stayed in a country cotage. For two weeks in Cornwall. It poured with rain neally every. Out of my bedroom window I could see a small boat bobbing up and down on the waves below. As I watched I suddenly saw a bright flare go up into the sky. I realised at once that the boat needed help.

A Underline the words you think could be improved. Choose a word of your own to put into the story instead. Also check the grammar, spelling and punctuation.

B On a separate sheet of paper, draft a second paragraph to continue the story. When you have finished the draft, see how you can improve it.

C Now write the whole story in your best handwriting on a sheet of paper.

Have all the corrections been made in **A**?	☐
Has the second paragraph been edited?	☐
Is there a difference in handwriting quality between **B** and **C**?	☐

Name _____ Date _____

Speedwriting

Write these words and then write the correct contraction.

	Words	**Contraction**
he will	he will	he'll
we will		
you will		
I am		
cannot		
she would		
he is		
do not		
you are		
they are		
we have		
they have		
it is		
does not		
could not		

Are the apostrophes at the right height and in the right place? ☐

Are the letters consistently spaced? ☐

Name _____ Date _____

Help to improve your handwriting by checking your own work. Make sure that:

1 You are forming your letters correctly.

2 Your letters are not too tall or too short.

3 Your descenders are not too long or too curly.

4 There are spaces between your letters.

5 There are spaces between your words.

6 Your down strokes are parallel.

7 Dots on letters **i** and **j** and crosses on **f** and **t** are placed correctly.

8 You are making all the joins correctly.

A Read through this nonsense rhyme. Write it out carefully.
Check your writing using the eight points above.

There was a young lady of Crete,
Who was so exceedingly neat,
When she got out of bed
She stood on her head,
To make sure of not soiling her feet.

‘A Young Lady of Crete’ (Anonymous)

B If you have made any mistakes, write the rhyme again on a sheet of paper.

Name _____   Date _____

Write these sentences.

Jessica's brother Tom invited seven friends to his birthday party.

They enjoyed swimming in the pool in the garden.

Jessica watched Tom pour water over their dad.

Tom gave balloons to his friends as they left.

Everyone said it had been a great party.

	sometimes	usually	always
Is your handwriting joined?	☐	☐	☐
Is your handwriting fluent?	☐	☐	☐
Is your handwriting legible?	☐	☐	☐

Nelson Handwriting Resources and Assessment Book 3 and Book 4 © Anita Warwick, Nelson Thornes Ltd, 2003

Name _____   Date _____

Write this poem on to plain paper. Remember to take care with your writing.

'Twas brillig, and the slithy toves
Did gyre and gimble in the wabe;
All mimsy were the borogroves,
And the mome raths outgrabe.

"Beware the Jabberwock, my son!
The jaws that bite, the claws that catch!
Beware the Jubjub bird, and shun
The frumious Bandersnatch!"

He took his vorpal sword in hand:
Long time the manxome foe he sought –
So rested he by the Tumtum tree,
And stood awhile in thought.

And as in uffish thought he stood,
The Jabberwock, with eyes of flame,
Came whiffling through the tulgey wood,
And burbled as it came!

One, two! One, two! And through and through
The vorpal blade went snicker-snack!
He left it dead, and with its head
He went galumphing back.

From *'**Jabberwocky**'* by *Lewis Carroll*

Are the letters formed correctly?

Are letters the correct size and height?

Is the spacing between letters and between words consistent?

Is the poem presented well?

Write this extract from **'King Lear'** by *William Shakespeare*.
Remember to slope your writing slightly to the right.

> Blow, winds, and crack your cheeks! Rage! Blow!
> You cataracts and hurricanes, spout
> Till you have drencht our steeples, drown'd the cocks!
> ... Things that love night
> Love not such nights as these; the wrathful skies
> Gallow the very wanderers of the dark,
> And make them keep their caves: Since I was man,
> Such sheets of fire, such bursts of horrid thunder,
> Such groans of roaring wind and rain, I never
> Remember to have heard ...

Are the letters formed correctly? ☐
Are letters the correct size and height? ☐
Is the spacing between letters and between words consistent? ☐
Is the extract presented well? ☐

Name _____   Date _____

Speedwriting

This is a reporter's finished article. Underline the main points in the article and then write the notes from which it was written.

I <u>arrived</u> at the scene of the fire at <u>10 o'clock</u> at <u>15 Brookside</u>. The <u>fire brigade arrived</u> at <u>10.05</u>. At 10.06 I saw flames coming through the roof. A woman appeared at an upstairs window and screamed. By 10.08 the fire-fighters were using hoses to fight the fire. A crowd had gathered. At 10.10 a ladder went up and a firefighter climbed it. At 10.12 he reached the upstairs window. Flames appeared behind the woman. At 10.13 the fire-fighter carried the woman down on his shoulders. She was put into an ambulance and taken to hospital.

_____

Notes

10.00 Arr. at fr.
15 Brksd.
10.05 Fr. brgd. arr.

Have useful contractions been made? ☐

Is the handwriting in an informal style? ☐

General Assessment

Book 4 Level

Name _____   Date _____

Presentation

Write this poem. Remember to think about how to present it neatly.

Beyond the wildest waves
and below the raging sea
sunk deep in the dark deep gloom
the guts of the Titanic
lie spilled on the ocean floor

lost in a battle of the swirls and swells
this mighty ship is stilled
its torn and twisted steel
wedged deep in the murky slime
as if crushed by a giant's fist

From *'The Titanic'* by *Andrea Lewis*

_____

_____

_____

_____

_____

_____

_____

_____

_____

Is the handwriting joined and legible? ☐

Is the poem presented neatly? ☐

     Nelson Handwriting Resources and Assessment Book 3 and Book 4 © Anita Warwick, Nelson Thornes Ltd, 2003

General Assessment

Book 4 Level

Name _____   Date _____

Drafting and editing

These are some notes taken from an article about water.

Use the notes to draft a full paragraph.

WATER

Water v precious, we oft. take it for granted.

U can drink, wash, cook, swim, fish in it.

Pple who live n countries where there isn't

enough cl water have a v dif time.

Has all the information from the notes been included? ☐

Does the paragraph make sense? ☐

Nelson Handwriting Resources and Assessment Book 3 and Book 4 © Anita Warwick, Nelson Thornes Ltd, 2003

General Assessment

Book 4 Level

Name _____   Date _____

Paragraphs

Read this passage about life in the country in Tudor times.

Country people often sang folk songs together in Tudor times. There were festivals on the village green. People played cards, dice, chess or draughts at home or in the inns. In the summer, villagers could practise archery, fishing or wrestling. Some people made their own musical instruments to play tunes for the singers. May 1st was a special festival day when people danced round the maypole. Football was played with a pig's bladder filled with air and it was a very rough game in those days. Travelling entertainers visited the villages to act out plays, and acrobats and jugglers also toured the countryside.

The information would be clearer as two paragraphs. Rewrite the passage so that information on outdoor sports is in one paragraph and information on other entertainments is in a second one. Use a separate sheet of paper. Remember to join your letters and to write neatly and fluently.

Are the paragraphs indented? ☐

Are the letters formed correctly? ☐

Are letters the correct size and height? ☐

Is the spacing between letters and between words consistent? ☐

Nelson Handwriting Resources and Assessment Book 3 and Book 4 © Anita Warwick, Nelson Thornes Ltd, 2003

Punctuation

Put the question marks, exclamation marks and apostrophes into these sentences.
Then write each sentence carefully.

"What is the matter" asked Gopal.

Dan said, "We cant find Toms ball."

"Can I watch television" asked Carl.

"Im very cross with you all" complained the
teacher.

"What an exciting day" sighed Darren.

"What time is the next train to Edinburgh"
Sonias Mum enquired.

Are the punctuation marks in the correct place? ☐
Are the punctuation marks spaced correctly? ☐
Is the handwriting neat and fluent? ☐

General Assessment

Book 4 Level

Name _____   Date _____

Break letters

A Copy this chart. Remember to leave a small space after a break letter.

hop	hopping	hopped
rub	rubbing	rubbed
drag	dragging	dragged
trap	trapping	trapped

B Choose the right form of the verb to complete each sentence. Then write the sentences.

The defender (trap) the ball.

Aladdin was (rub) the lamp.

He (drag) the heavy load.

The rabbit (hop) into the garden.

Is there a consistent space before and after each break letter? ☐

Is the handwriting fluent and legible? ☐

Self-assessment

Name _____   Date _____

A Write this passage carefully but not too slowly.

When writing a word, the spacing between your letters should look even. Don't squash your letters (especially if you are at the end of a line) or space them too far apart. You should be able to pencil in a letter **o** between words. Practice in writing will help you to become a better writer only if you keep trying to improve your letters and to write quickly, neatly and rhythmically.

B Look carefully at what you have written.

Are your letters the correct shape, size and height? ☐

Is there a consistent and correct space between
your letters and between your words? ☐

Are you joining your letters correctly? ☐

C Practise the letters, joins and words that you wrote least well. Then write the passage again. Try to write quickly but steadily and well.

Self-assessment

Book 4 Level

Name _____   Date _____

Help to improve your handwriting by checking your own work. Make sure that:

1 Your writing forms straight lines across the page. ☐
2 Spaces between letters, words and lines are regular. ☐
3 Your down strokes are parallel. ☐
4 Letters are neither too tall nor too short. ☐
5 Tails on letters are not too long. ☐
6 Dots on the letters **i** and **j** are placed correctly. ☐
7 Cross strokes on the letters **f** and **t** are placed correctly. ☐
8 All joins are made correctly. ☐

A Read the nonsense rhyme below. Write it out carefully. Check your writing using the eight points above.

> As I was walking up the stair
> I met a man who wasn't there;
> He wasn't there again today.
> I wish, I wish he'd stay away.

*'**The Little Man**' by Hughes Mearns*

_____

_____

_____

_____

B If you have made any mistakes, write the rhyme again on a sheet of paper. Try not to make any mistakes at all this time.

C Now try writing the rhyme as quickly as you can on a sheet of paper. Make sure your writing is legible.

Name _____ Date _____

Words that have a short vowel before ending in a single consonant double the consonant before adding **ing** or **ed**.

Copy these words.

hum	humming	hummed
hug	hugging	hugged
beg	begging	begged
pot	potting	potted
wrap	wrapping	wrapped
trap	trapping	trapped

Ensuring letters are consistent in height and size.

Nelson Handwriting Resources and Assessment Book 3 and Book 4 © Anita Warwick, Nelson Thornes Ltd, 2003

Name _____ Date _____

A Read this passage.

Gale Warning!

When the air moves about we say that the wind is blowing. Sometimes the air moves slowly and we get a gentle breeze. Sometimes it moves very quickly and storms and hurricanes occur.

In 1805, a British admiral called Sir Francis Beaufort worked out what happened at sea when the air moved at different speeds. The Beaufort Scale was adapted for the effects of wind on land and is still in use today.

B Copy the passage. Make sure your letters are consistent in height and size.

_____

_____

_____

_____

_____

_____

_____

_____

_____

Ensuring letters are consistent in height and size.

Nelson Handwriting Resources and Assessment Book 3 and Book 4 © Anita Warwick, Nelson Thornes Ltd, 2003

Name _____ Date _____

When we write about strong feelings, we use an exclamation mark instead of a full stop. The exclamation mark is written before the closing speech mark, like this:

"Wow!" said Jason. "Look at that car."

Exclamation marks are the same height as capital letters. Fill in the missing exclamation marks in these sentences. Write the correct sentences.

1 *"Help Help" cried the sailors.*

_____

2 *"Look out" shouted the captain.*

_____

3 *"What an exciting day" said Darren.*

_____

4 *"I'm very cross with you" Mum shouted.*

_____

5 *"Be careful" exclaimed Sarah.*

_____

Practising with punctuation.

Nelson Handwriting Resources and Assessment Book 3 and Book 4 © Anita Warwick, Nelson Thornes Ltd, 2003

Name _____ Date _____

An apostrophe looks like a comma, but it is the same height as an ascender. It shows that a letter or letters have been left out of a word *or* that someone owns something, like this:

I didn't want it. (The letter **o** has been left out.)

That is John's dinner. (The dinner belongs to John.)

A Copy these sentences. Add an apostrophe where a letter or letters have been left out.

1 _Now were getting somewhere._

2 _That wasnt a very good idea._

3 _Hes running very fast._

4 _I think well still be late._

B Copy these sentences. Add an apostrophe to show that someone owns something.

1 _The cat is Dans pet._

2 _Emilys perfect pet is a guinea pig._

3 _We thought the guinea pigs name was Lucy._

4 _But Lucy is the cats name!_

Practising with punctuation.

Nelson Handwriting Resources and Assessment Book 3 and Book 4 © Anita Warwick, Nelson Thornes Ltd, 2003

Name _____ Date _____

A Break letters do not join. Copy the break letters.

b   p   g   q   j   x   y   z

B Most nouns ending in **o** form their plural by adding **s**. Copy these singular and plural words.

yoyo   yoyos

banjo   banjos

bongo   bongos

zero   zeros

zoo   zoos

igloo   igloos

patio   patios

piano   pianos

gecko   geckos

Practising break letters.

Nelson Handwriting Resources and Assessment Book 3 and Book 4 © Anita Warwick, Nelson Thornes Ltd, 2003

Extension Resource

Book 3

Nelson

Name _____ Date _____

Handwriting

A Write each word on the line below it.

Definition

banjo _____

_____

bongo _____

_____

gecko _____

_____

matzo _____

_____

yoyo _____

_____

piazza _____

_____

pizza _____

_____

samba _____

_____

puma _____

_____

pagoda _____

_____

B Look up each word in a dictionary and write the definition beside it.

Practising break letters.

Nelson Handwriting Resources and Assessment Book 3 and Book 4 © Anita Warwick, Nelson Thornes Ltd, 2003

Name _____ Date _____

The prefix **auto** means 'self'. Copy these words. Remember to use the diagonal joining line to join from the letter **m**. This will help to make sure there is a space between your letters.

automat

automate

automatic

automatically

automation

automaton

automobile

automotive

autonomous

autonomy

Practising joining from the letter **m**.

unit **4**

Name _____ Date _____

Copy these verses on to a sheet of paper in your best handwriting.
Arrange your page attractively with good margins and some decoration.

The Owl and the Pussy-cat went to sea
In a beautiful pea-green boat,
They took some honey and plenty of money,
Wrapped up in a five-pound note.

The Owl looked up to the stars above,
And sang to a small guitar,
"O lovely Pussy! O Pussy, my love,
What a beautiful Pussy you are,
You are,
You are!
What a beautiful Pussy you are!"

From *'The Owl and the Pussy-cat'* by *Edward Lear*

Practising joining from the letter **m**.

Name _____ Date _____

The prefix **inter** means 'between'. Add **inter** to each word and write the new word two or three times. The first one is done to help you.

act   *interact*   *interact*   *interact*

active

change

connect

face

lock

mission

mix

national

relate

view

weave

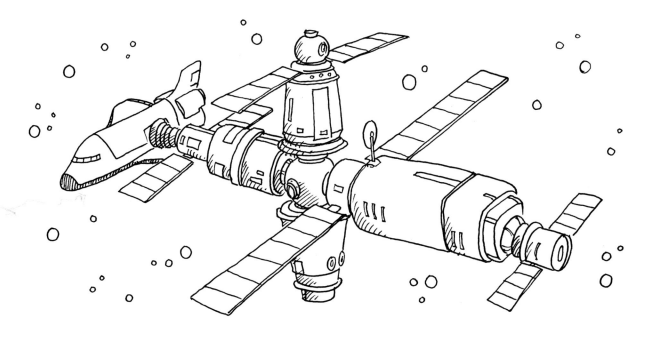

Ensuring the letter **t** is not as tall as other letters with an ascender.

Nelson Handwriting Resources and Assessment Book 3 and Book 4 © Anita Warwick, Nelson Thornes Ltd, 2003

Name _____ Date _____

Copy this passage. Remember to make sure the letter **t** is not as tall as other letters with an ascender.

The First Steps on the Moon

   The door of the Apollo 11 lunar module opened and Neil Armstrong emerged. He carried a backpack containing enough oxygen for four hours. Armstrong unveiled a television camera so the world could witness his first step. "That's one small step for a man, and one giant leap for mankind," he said. It was 21 July 1969. All around the world people marvelled at this great achievement and wondered what the next step would be.

Ensuring the letter **t** is not as tall as other letters with an ascender.

Nelson Handwriting Resources and Assessment Book 3 and Book 4 © Anita Warwick, Nelson Thornes Ltd, 2003

Focus Resource

Book 3

Nelson
Handwriting

Name _____ Date _____

Letters within words must only touch each other with a joining line. The joining line helps to make sure there is a space between the letters.

A Copy the suffix **tion**. Join your letters carefully.

tion   tion

B Copy these words. Underline the suffix **tion**.

direction

fiction

attention

proportion

C Copy the suffix **sion**. Remember to space your letters neatly.

sion   sion

D Copy these words. Underline the suffix **sion**.

collision

confusion

explosion

exclusion

Practising spacing within words.

Nelson Handwriting Resources and Assessment Book 3 and Book 4 © Anita Warwick, Nelson Thornes Ltd, 2003

unit 6

Extension Resource

Book 3

Nelson
Handwriting

Name _____ Date _____

- selling by telephone
- device for transmitting messages
- apparatus for transmitting sound (especially speech)
- message sent by telegraph and delivered in printed form
- message sent by telephone or telex and delivered in printed form
- communication by telegraph

Write the correct definition from the box above next to each word. Remember to leave the correct space between the letters in your words. The first one is done to help you.

Definition

telephone — *apparatus for transmitting sound (especially speech)*

telegram

telegraph

telegraphy

telemessage

telesales

Practising spacing within words.

Nelson Handwriting Resources and Assessment Book 3 and Book 4 © Anita Warwick, Nelson Thornes Ltd, 2003

Name _____ Date _____

Most words just add **s** in the plural. Add an **s** to make each of these words plural and write the new words two or three times. The first one is done to help you.

car   cars   cars   cars

bicycle

school

cinema

camera

tourist

park

palace

museum

theatre

boat

Developing fluency.

Nelson Handwriting Resources and Assessment Book 3 and Book 4 © Anita Warwick, Nelson Thornes Ltd, 2003

Name _____ Date _____

Copy this poem on to a sheet of plain paper.

BALLOONING OVER LONDON

The mist has cleared and far below
We see the snake-like river flow.

And though it's huge, the London Eye
Looks like a toy from way up high.

There's Nelson's Column – and dare we scare
The hordes of pigeons in Trafalgar Square?

We hover an hour (the air's not chilly)
Then pick up speed over Piccadilly.

Now hold on tight – we're drifting down
Above the Thames that runs through town.

Back where we started – who would have thought?
We land with a bump at Hampton Court!

By *Ronald Kay*

Developing fluency.

Nelson Handwriting Resources and Assessment Book 3 and Book 4 © Anita Warwick, Nelson Thornes Ltd, 2003

Name _____ Date _____

Stand back and let the better man cross!

I AM the better man, so get out of my way!

The story in a play is told through the speeches of the characters.
The speeches are set out like this:

ROBIN: *Stand back and let the better*
                     man cross!

STRANGER: *I AM the better man, so get out*
                     of my way!

Copy the next part of the play.

ROBIN: *You talk like a coward.*

STRANGER: *I am no coward.*

_____

_____

Practising writing a playscript.

Nelson Handwriting Resources and Assessment Book 3 and Book 4 © Anita Warwick, Nelson Thornes Ltd, 2003

unit **8**

Extension Resource

Book 3

Nelson

Handwriting

Name _____ Date _____

Three members of a football team wanted to buy a new strip for the team. They discussed how to raise the money and decided on a garage sale. They asked their teammates to collect second-hand toys and sports equipment. James' parents agreed to let them have the sale in their garage. The three team members raised enough money to buy a new strip for everyone in the team.

Make up a playscript for this story to show how the children organised the garage sale and what happened. The script has been started for you.

The Garage Sale

JAMES: I think our team needs a new strip.

SAM: Bright green with a black collar and black sleeves would look good.

SEAN: We'll need a lot of money. How can we get it?

Continue on a sheet of paper if necessary.

Practising writing a playscript.

Nelson Handwriting Resources and Assessment Book 3 and Book 4 © Anita Warwick, Nelson Thornes Ltd, 2003

Name _____ Date _____

Use small print to write the names of some of the countries Amy Johnson flew over on her solo flight to Sydney.

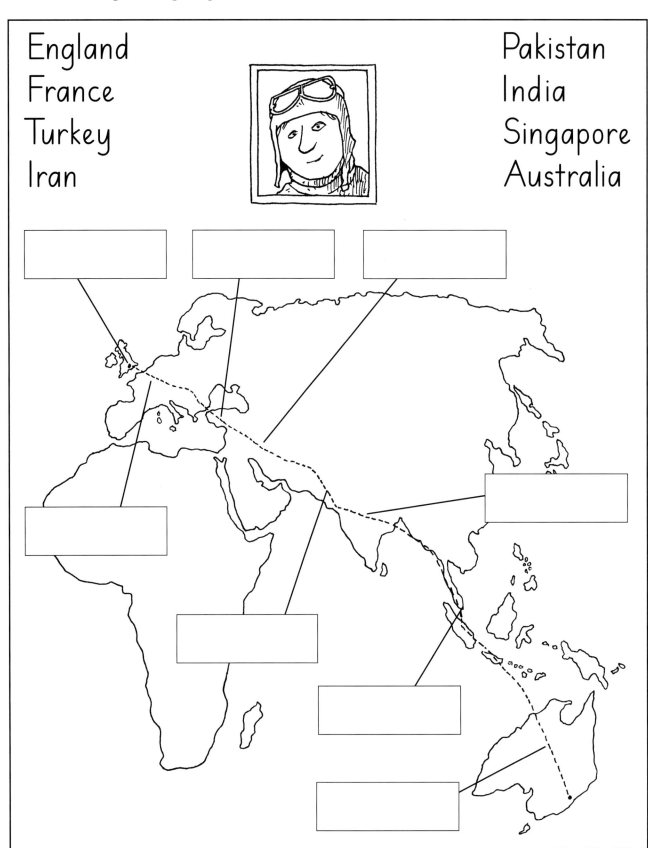

England
France
Turkey
Iran

Pakistan
India
Singapore
Australia

Practising printing.

Nelson Handwriting Resources and Assessment Book 3 and Book 4 © Anita Warwick, Nelson Thornes Ltd, 2003

Name _____ Date _____

A Print these instructions on to a sheet of paper.

How to Make a Compass

Equipment needed: a bar magnet, string, paper, tape
1 Tie one end of the string around the magnet.
2 Fix the string to the edge of a table.
3 Draw a large circle marked N, S, W, E on the paper.
4 Place the paper under the magnet.
5 Turn the paper so that the magnet points to N.
6 Tape the paper to the floor.

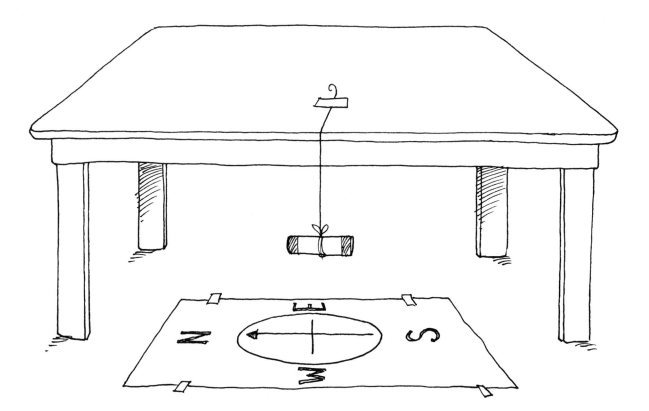

B Use your compass to find out which way the classroom windows face.

C Give your instructions to a friend in another class. See if your friend can follow the instructions.

Practising printing.

Nelson Handwriting Resources and Assessment Book 3 and Book 4 © Anita Warwick, Nelson Thornes Ltd, 2003

Name _____ Date _____

Many nouns that end in **f** drop the **f** and add **ves** in the plural form. Write the
singular form of these words three times. The first one is done to help you.

calves   _calf_   _calf_   _calf_

halves

thieves

leaves

loaves

scarves

wolves

Practising forming and joining the letter **f**.

Nelson Handwriting Resources and Assessment Book 3 and Book 4 © Anita Warwick, Nelson Thornes Ltd, 2003

Name _____ Date _____

Copy this poem line by line.

FLY A FLAG

Fly a flag, float a boat,

Brush the fluff off your coat;

Get some flour, bake a cake,

Eat a giant chocolate flake;

Put on flip-flops, mop the floor –

But mind the flowerpot by the door!

By *Ronald Kay*

Practising forming and joining the letter **f**.

Nelson Handwriting Resources and Assessment Book 3 and Book 4 © Anita Warwick, Nelson Thornes Ltd, 2003

unit 11

Focus Resource

Book 3

Nelson

Handwriting

Name _____ Date _____

Copy this poem into the frame below it. Complete the pattern on the frame.

Reading
Way of learning
Source of fun and leisure
Gateway to a thousand pleasures
Super

Practising presentation.

Nelson Handwriting Resources and Assessment Book 3 and Book 4 © Anita Warwick, Nelson Thornes Ltd, 2003

Name _____ Date _____

Copy this poem on to plain paper. Use your neatest handwriting. Decorate the poem with a border.

RAINY NIGHTS

I like the town on rainy nights
When everything is wet –
When all the town has magic lights
And streets of shining jet!

When all the rain about the town
Is like a looking-glass,
And all the lights are upside-down
Below me as I pass.

In all the pools are velvet skies,
And down the dazzling street
A fairy city gleams and lies
In beauty at my feet.

By *Irene Thompson*

Practising presentation.

Nelson Handwriting Resources and Assessment Book 3 and Book 4 © Anita Warwick, Nelson Thornes Ltd, 2003

Copy this shape poem on to plain paper. Make sure the poem fits into an apple shape.

FRUIT SALAD

Apples
make cider
Bananas - milk shake
Oranges - squash
Plums - tummy ache
Gooseberries bake
Green frogspawn pie
but brambles
paint fingers
like bruises
with dye

Pears
cry in drops
Round raspberry cake
Sliced lemon swims
in a lemonade lake
Strawberries quake
in jelly and jam
but tomato's
the fruit that
tastes best
with ham

By *Gina Douthwaite*

Practising writing shape poems.

Name _____ Date _____

Copy this shape poem on to plain paper.

POLLUTION

SMOKE SMOKE SMOKE SMOOO
SMOKE SMOKE SMOKE SMOOO

DUST
GRIT
ACID
RAIN
BLOW
WIND
KILL
MAIM
DRIP
LEAK
FALL
RAIN
ATOM
BOMB
BURN
FLAME
CREEPING CRAWLING
OOZING SEEPING
SMELLING SWELLING
WAILING WEEPING
TECHNOLOGICALLY SPEAKING
PROGRESS IS ITS NAME. . . . . . .

Practising writing shape poems.

Nelson Handwriting Resources and Assessment Book 3 and Book 4 © Anita Warwick, Nelson Thornes Ltd, 2003

Name _____ Date _____

A Copy these letters neatly.

a b c d e f g h i j k l m n o p q r s t u v w x y z

A B C D E F G H I J K L M

N O P Q R S T U V W X Y Z

B Print the name and address of the publisher of this book.

Nelson Thornes Ltd

Delta Place

27 Bath Road

Cheltenham

GL53 7TH

C Print your school address.

D Now print your home address.

Practising printing.

Nelson Handwriting Resources and Assessment Book 3 and Book 4 © Anita Warwick, Nelson Thornes Ltd, 2003

Name _____ Date _____

A Copy these signs neatly. Use the print alphabet.

Post Office   Police Station   Railway Station

Fire Station   Health Centre

Hospital   Pharmacy   Ambulance Station

Supermarket   Baker   Health Centre

Leisure Centre   Park   Museum

Restaurant   Hotel   Newsagent   Swimming Pool

B Print eight more notices that you might see in your local environment.

1 _____   2 _____

3 _____   4 _____

5 _____   6 _____

7 _____   8 _____

Practising printing.

Nelson Handwriting Resources and Assessment Book 3 and Book 4 © Anita Warwick, Nelson Thornes Ltd, 2003

Name _____ Date _____

A Practise writing these patterns until you can write them evenly, smoothly and quickly. Use plain paper.

vvvvvvvvvvvvv   uuuuuuuuuuuuu

eeeeeeeeeeeeeeeee   ccccccccccc

B Copy these words. Add **ing** to each word. Then add **ed** or **er** to each word. (Remember to double the consonant.) The first one is done to help you.

		Add **ing**	Add **ed** or **er**
dig	dig	digging	digger
drag			
drop			
mop			
stop			
hug			
hum			
run			
beg			
fit			

Practising speedwriting.

Nelson Handwriting Resources and Assessment Book 3 and Book 4 © Anita Warwick, Nelson Thornes Ltd, 2003

Name _____ Date _____

A Practise writing these patterns on plain paper. Gradually increase your speed.

wwwwww   ccccccccc   VVVVVVV

B Copy this sentence. Try to improve the smoothness and steadiness of your writing as well as its speed.

The pen should move smoothly and steadily

from letter to letter and from word to word.

C When you write, your hand has to move gradually across the page. Copy this sentence. Move your hand at a steady speed with no jerky movements.

The speed of writing increases as the smoothness and

steadiness of writing movements improve with practice.

D Find your writing speed. Divide the number of letters written by the number of minutes taken, like this:

$$\frac{\text{Number of letters written}}{\text{Number of minutes taken}} = \text{writing speed (in letters per minute)}$$

Record your score here.

My writing speed is ⬚ letters per minute.

Practising speedwriting.

Nelson Handwriting Resources and Assessment Book 3 and Book 4 © Anita Warwick, Nelson Thornes Ltd, 2003

Name _____ Date _____

A Flourishes are often used to decorate capital letters. Copy these examples.

A B C D E F G H I J K L M N

O P Q R S T U V W X Y Z

B Look carefully at this acrostic. There are words that can be read from left to right, right to left, down from the top and up from the bottom. Write the acrostic in decorated capital letters.

R O T A S
O P E R A
T E N E T
A R E P O
S A T O R

_____

_____

_____

_____

_____

C Use decorated capital letters to write some of your friends' names.

_____

_____

_____

Practising writing decorated capital letters.

Nelson Handwriting Resources and Assessment Book 3 and Book 4 © Anita Warwick, Nelson Thornes Ltd, 2003

Name _____ Date _____

A A page of well-presented writing can be made even more attractive by decorating the capital letters. Copy this style of decorated capitals.

A B C D E F G H I J K L M

N O P Q R S T U V W X Y Z

B Use the style of decorated capitals above to write the names of these famous buildings.

THE WHITE HOUSE

THE TAJ MAHAL

THE ALBERT HALL

THE EIFFEL TOWER

SYDNEY OPERA HOUSE

Practising writing decorated capital letters.

Nelson Handwriting Resources and Assessment Book 3 and Book 4 © Anita Warwick, Nelson Thornes Ltd, 2003

Focus Resource

unit 16

Book 3

Nelson
Handwriting

Name _____ Date _____

Copy this letter on to a sheet of paper in your best handwriting. Put guidelines underneath. Notice how the letter is set out.

17 Wheatsheaf Lane,
Southdell AL4 7BC
15th August 2003

Dear Alex,

    One of my friends owns a hot-air balloon. He has invited me to go with him on a flight over the countryside. He plans to go on Saturday, and says that you are invited too. Would you like to come? Ask your parents if you can come and let me know by Friday evening.

    Love to everyone,
    Uncle John

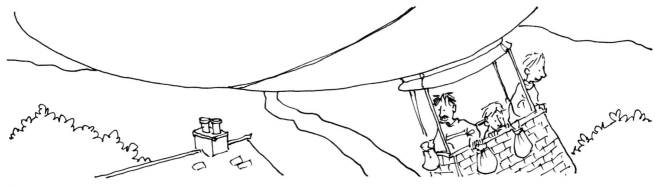

Practising writing letters.

Nelson Handwriting Resources and Assessment Book 3 and Book 4 © Anita Warwick, Nelson Thornes Ltd, 2003

Name _____ Date _____

A newspaper has invited children to write a letter about their favourite television programme. The writer of the best letter will win tickets to see the programme being recorded. Write a letter about your favourite programme. Use the letter below as a starting point. Remember to put in your address and the date.

Dear Sir,

    My name is   and I am   years old. I will try my hardest to write a good letter as I would really love to win this competition and go to see my favourite programme being recorded.

Practising writing letters.

Nelson Handwriting Resources and Assessment Book 3 and Book 4 © Anita Warwick, Nelson Thornes Ltd, 2003

Name _____ Date _____

A Copy this paragraph neatly. Remember to indent the first word.

Looking After a Dog
*   A pet dog needs regular meals and clean water to drink. Its diet should include meat, biscuits and vegetables. Tinned and dried dog food provide all these. A dog also needs plenty of exercise and regular grooming and it must, of course, be house-trained.*

_____

_____

_____

_____

_____

_____

B Now write a paragraph about looking after a cat or another pet. Use a separate sheet of paper. Remember to indent the first word.

Practising paragraphs.

Nelson Handwriting Resources and Assessment Book 3 and Book 4 © Anita Warwick, Nelson Thornes Ltd, 2003

Extension Resource

Book 3

Nelson

Handwriting

Name _____ Date _____

Rewrite this information as two paragraphs.

Nicholas Fisk has written around 40 books, including many science-fiction titles for older children. He completed his first book when he was only nine years old! He has tried many different jobs including acting and playing jazz, but he likes writing best. However, Nicholas Fisk doesn't like his books to be labelled as sci-fi. He says his books are written from the point of view of 'If...' because then anything can happen in them. He enjoys writing for young people because they find it easier than adults to accept the unconventional.

Practising paragraphs with indentation.

Nelson Handwriting Resources and Assessment Book 3 and Book 4 © Anita Warwick, Nelson Thornes Ltd, 2003

Name _____ Date _____

Copy this limerick into the frame below it. Complete the pattern on the frame.

THERE WAS A YOUNG LADY OF RIGA

There was a young lady of Riga
Who rode with a smile on a tiger,
They returned from the ride,
With the lady inside,
And the smile on the face of the tiger.

(Anonymous)

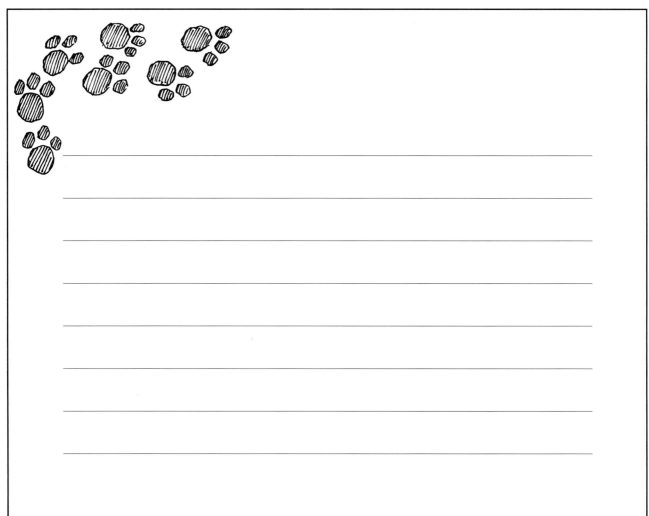

Practising presentation.

Copy this poem carefully on to plain paper. Notice the shape of the poem.
Does it remind you of the way seals move?

SEAL

See how he dives
From the rocks with a zoom!
See how he darts
Through his watery room,
Past crabs and eels
And green seaweed,
Past fluffs of sandy
Minnow feed!
See how he swims
With a swerve and a twist,
A flip of the flipper,
A flick of the wrist!
Quicksilver-quick,
Softer than spray,
Down he plunges
And sweeps away.

By *William Jay Smith*

Practising presentation.

Name _____ Date _____

A Copy these words.

live	lived	lively
love	loved	lovely
brave	braved	bravely

B Drop the final **e** and then add the suffix **ed** to these words.
Write each new word three times.

care

stare

share

C Drop the final **e** and then add the suffix **ing** to these words.
Write each new word three times.

weave

welcome

wedge

Revising difficult joins.

Name _____ Date _____

Copy this poem carefully.

THE SEEDLING

An old man was planting a seedling

Of a great oak tree to be;

His son asked him, "Why are you working

For something you never will see?"

His father replied, "As I look around

I see tree after tree after tree;

So now I am doing for your children

What my ancestors did for me!"

By Ronald Kay

Revising difficult joins.

Nelson Handwriting Resources and Assessment Book 3 and Book 4 © Anita Warwick, Nelson Thornes Ltd, 2003

Name _____ Date _____

A Copy this rhyme in your usual handwriting style.

A blink, I think, is the same as a wink,
A blink is a wink that grew,
For a wink you blink with only one eye,
For a blink you wink with two.

By *Jacqueline Segal*

_____

_____

_____

_____

Some people develop their writing by adding loops to **f**, **g**, **j** and **y**.

A blink, I think, is the same as a wink,
A blink is a wink that grew,
For a wink you blink with only one eye,
For a blink you wink with two.

B Now try writing the rhyme with loops.

_____

_____

_____

_____

Looking at different handwriting styles.

Nelson Handwriting Resources and Assessment Book 3 and Book 4 © Anita Warwick, Nelson Thornes Ltd, 2003

Name _____ Date _____

A Copy this poem on to a sheet of paper in your usual handwriting style.

HUMPTY DUMPTY WENT TO THE MOON

Humpty Dumpty went to the moon
On a supersonic spoon.
He took some porridge and a tent
But when he landed
The spoon got bent.
Humpty said he didn't care
And for all I know
He's still up there.

By *Michael Rosen*

Some people develop their handwriting by adding loops to **f**, **g**, **j** and **y**
and joining from **b** and **p**, like this:

HUMPTY DUMPTY WENT TO THE MOON

Humpty Dumpty went to the moon
On a supersonic spoon.
He took some porridge and a tent
But when he landed
The spoon got bent.
Humpty said he didn't care
And for all I know
He's still up there.

B Copy this version of the poem on to another
sheet of paper. Make sure you add the loops
and the joins from **b** and **p**.

Looking at different handwriting styles.

Nelson Handwriting Resources and Assessment Book 3 and Book 4 © Anita Warwick, Nelson Thornes Ltd, 2003

Name _____ Date _____

A For sloped writing you need to angle your paper slightly. Practise writing these patterns and letters with a slight slope to the right.

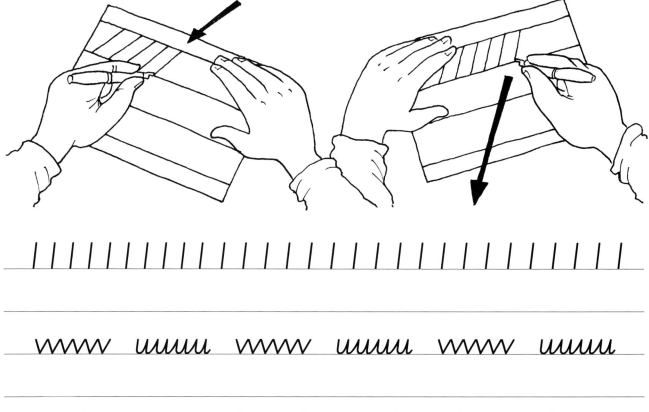

| | | | | | | | | | | | | | | | | | | | | | | | | | | | | | | | | | | | | | | | | | | | |

vvvvv uuuuu vvvvv uuuuu vvvvv uuuuu

mnhmnh mnhmnh mnhmnh mnhmnh

B Copy these prefixes and words.

bi binary biped binoculars

tele telephone telegram telescope

aqua aquarium aquaplane aquatic

Revising sloped writing.

Nelson Handwriting Resources and Assessment Book 3 and Book 4 © Anita Warwick, Nelson Thornes Ltd, 2003

Name _____ Date _____

A Copy the lower-case letters three times. Try to slope your writing slightly to the right.

a b c d e f g h i j k l m n o p q r s t u v w x y z

B Copy the joins three times.

an ip sc ub om we rs ch el dr ll wl vh ob

C Copy the capital letters three times.

A B C D E F G H I J K L M N O P Q R S T U V W X Y Z

Revising sloped writing.

Nelson Handwriting Resources and Assessment Book 3 and Book 4 © Anita Warwick, Nelson Thornes Ltd, 2003

Name _____ Date _____

Practise writing these patterns and letters, making sure they are consistent in height and size.

mmmmmmmm   mmmmmmmm   mmmmmmmm

n n n n n n   nnnnnnnnnn   n n n n n

m m m m m   mmmmmmm   m m m m m

h h h h h h   hhhhhhhhhh   h h h h h h

k k k k k k k   kkkkkkkkkkk   k k k k k k k

uuuuuuuuuu   uuuuuuuuuu   uuuuuuuuuu

u u u u u u u   uuuuuuuuuuuu   u u u u u u u

yyyyyyyyyy yyyyyyyyyy gggggggggg gggggggggg

qqqqqqqqqq qqqqqqqqq ppppppppp ppppppppp

ttttttttttt ttttttttttt fffffffffff fffffffffff

Ensuring letters are the correct height and size.

Nelson Handwriting Resources and Assessment Book 3 and Book 4 © Anita Warwick, Nelson Thornes Ltd, 2003

Name _____ Date _____

Copy this poem. Make sure your letters are consistent in height and size.

POEM POWER

In matters of battle why take to the gun?

Just write a few poems – it's safer, and fun!

No-one gets killed or injured for life –

It's a much saner way to counteract strife!

A combat of verses decides who's the winner –

And it all could take place in a room after dinner!

By *Ronald Kay*

Ensuring letters are the correct height and size.

Name _____ Date _____

A Copy these words. Make sure you leave the correct space between your letters. Remember that joining your letters correctly helps you to leave a space between them.

fattening   *astronomy*   *dandelion*

holiday   *parliament*   *mathematics*

definite   *separate*   *January*

medicine   *Saturday*   *lemonade*

describe   *jewellery*   *geography*

February   *telephone*   *television*

B Underline the unstressed vowels. The first ones are done to help you.

Practising spacing.

Name _____ Date _____

When writing down exactly what is spoken, we use speech marks to show the beginning and end of the direct speech.

Copy these sentences. Leave the correct space between letters and the correct space between words. Add the commas, full stops and speech marks, like this:

Grace yelled, "I can see some survivors."

1 *Dad, keep rowing shouted Grace*

2 *How much further is it? asked her father*

3 *We're nearly there exclaimed Grace*

4 *Thank you for saving us sobbed the survivors*

5 *Three of you sit at the front said Grace and the rest sit behind me*

6 *Dad, I know it's hard said Grace but we're nearly home*

Practising spacing.

Nelson Handwriting Resources and Assessment Book 3 and Book 4 © Anita Warwick, Nelson Thornes Ltd, 2003

Name _____ Date _____

A Reporters have to write quickly. They often use notes. This is a reporter's finished article about the sinking of the *Titanic* in 1912. Underline the main points in the article.

> Mʀ C.H. Sᴛᴇɴɢᴀʟ, a <u>first-class</u> <u>passenger</u> who was on board the *Titanic* the night it sank, said that when the *Titanic* <u>struck</u> the <u>iceberg</u> the <u>impact</u> was <u>terrific</u>, and great <u>blocks</u> of <u>ice</u> were <u>thrown on</u> the <u>deck</u>, killing a number of people. The stern of the vessel rose in the air, and people ran shrieking from their berths below. Women and children were quickly placed in boats by the sailors, who like their officers, it was stated, were heard to threaten that they would shoot male passengers if they attempted to get in the boats ahead of the women. Indeed, it was said that shots were actually heard.

B Write the notes from which the article was written. The first ones are done to help you.

Mr C H Stengal 1st cls pass

Titanic struck iceberg impact terrific

blocks ice thrown on dck

Practising speedwriting.

Nelson Handwriting Resources and Assessment Book 3 and Book 4 © Anita Warwick, Nelson Thornes Ltd, 2003

Name _____ Date _____

Copy this passage quickly but neatly.

At 12.30 a.m. on 4 April 2001 the ship, lost power
in both her engines and began to float helplessly towards
the rocks. The wind was blowing at gale force. Waves
over 25 metres high were crashing over the ship. At
12.40 a.m. a terrific bang was heard. The ship had hit
a rock and there was a large hole in her side. Water
began to pour into the hull as the passengers and crew
ran towards the lifeboats. At 1.00 a.m. a helicopter
arrived at the scene and began to winch the passengers
and crew to safety. Miraculously, everyone survived.

Practising speedwriting.

Nelson Handwriting Resources and Assessment Book 3 and Book 4 © Anita Warwick, Nelson Thornes Ltd, 2003

Name _____ Date _____

A Read this first draft of a paragraph about Isambard Kingdom Brunel.
Underline the spelling mistakes.

In 1836 Brunel began bilting what was to become the bigest steamship in the world at that time. The ship was called the 'Great Western' and she was desined to cross the Atlantic Ocen. However, on her first voyage the ship cauht fire and Brunel fel down a deep hatch as he rushd to put out the blase. The 'Great Western' wnt on to cros the Atlantic in forteen and a halve days.

B Write the correct spellings below. Use a dictionary to help you.

_____

_____

_____

_____

_____

C Write the paragraph again on a sheet of paper in your best handwriting. Use the
correct spellings. Remember to slope your writing slightly to the right.

Practising drafting and editing.

Nelson Handwriting Resources and Assessment Book 3 and Book 4 © Anita Warwick, Nelson Thornes Ltd, 2003

A This is the first draft of a short biography of Charles Darwin. Correct the words that are spelt wrongly.

Charles Darwin was born in 1809. He spnt most of his live searching for the truth about the world threw careful observation of nature. At the age of twenty-one he set of round the world as the official naturalist on a ship called the 'Beagle'. The voyage lasted fife years.

He was fassinated by the extraordinary animals he saw and made a great collection of specimens to take home, including the fossilised bones of enormous animals that had died out long ago.

In 1859 Darwin published a book called 'The Origin of the Species'. His theory of evolution through natural selection completely changed our way of loking at the world but it also caused an uproar at the time. The idea of evolution was not knew in the 1850s. People had realised that animals and plants had changed over thousands of years. But Darwin's theory seemed to sugest that humans were descended directly from apes. Darwin died in 1882.

B Write a final draft on to a sheet of paper in your best handwriting. Use your correction marks to help you replace the words that are spelt wrongly.

Practising drafting and editing.

Nelson Handwriting Resources and Assessment Book 3 and Book 4 © Anita Warwick, Nelson Thornes Ltd, 2003

Name _____ Date _____

Copy this alphabet shape poem. Make sure your capital letters are the same height as letters with an ascender.

ALPHABET STORY

A
  Big
     Cat
       Dashed
         Excitedly
        For
        Gertie
      Hedgehog
   In
  Janet's
Kitchen
  Last
    Monday
     Night.
      Only
       Peter,
       Quietly
     Reading,
   Saw
  The
Unwelcome
  Visitors.
   "Why,
    Xena –
     You're
      Z
       i   g g i
        g a   n
         z   g!"

By *Ronald Kay*

Practising writing capital letters.

Nelson Handwriting Resources and Assessment Book 3 and Book 4 © Anita Warwick, Nelson Thornes Ltd, 2003

Name _____ Date _____

On 28 July 1857, a national newspaper described the Grand Military Festival that had been organised to raise money to help Mary Seacole.

Copy this extract. Insert the missing capital letters.

few names were more familiar to the public during the crimea war than that of mrs seacole. at the end of both the first half and the second half of the festival her name was shouted by a thousand voices. never did a woman seem happier, and never was such a hearty and kindly greeting bestowed upon a worthier object.

Practising writing capital letters.

Nelson Handwriting Resources and Assessment Book 3 and Book 4 © Anita Warwick, Nelson Thornes Ltd, 2003

Name _____ Date _____

These seven verbs all end with a consonant plus **e**. Before adding **ed** or **ing**, the final **e** is dropped.

gaze   chuckle   injure   charge
decide   advertise   mumble

Choose the correct verb to complete each sentence. Change the ending to **ed** or **ing**. Copy the sentences, writing quickly, fluently and legibly.

1 We all _____ at the joke.

2 Television stations are always _____ cars.

3 We could not hear because the actor was _____.

4 The baby was _____ up at her mother.

5 The referee _____ that it was too foggy to play.

6 Tom was badly _____ when he fell.

7 A huge elephant came _____ at the keeper.

_____

_____

_____

_____

_____

_____

_____

Practising fluency.

Nelson Handwriting Resources and Assessment Book 3 and Book 4 © Anita Warwick, Nelson Thornes Ltd, 2003

Extension Resource

Book 4

Name _____ Date _____

Nelson
Handwriting

Copy this poem. Remember to join your letters. Sloping your writing slightly to the right will help you write quickly and fluently.

IF THINGS GREW DOWN

If things grew down instead of up,
A dog would grow into a pup.
A cat would grow into a kitten,
Your sweater would grow into a mitten.
A cow would grow into a calf,
And a whole would grow into a half.
Big would grow into something small.
And small would grow into nothing at all.

By *Robert D. Hoeft*

Practising fluency.

Nelson Handwriting Resources and Assessment Book 3 and Book 4 © Anita Warwick, Nelson Thornes Ltd, 2003

Name _____ Date _____

Copy this paragraph neatly. Remember to indent the first word.

The pyramids of Giza are guarded by a huge sphinx. This massive stone statue of a lion has the head of a man, who may be the pharaoh Khafra. The Great Sphinx was probably built on Khafra's orders. It looks east, towards the rising sun. For most of the last 4,500 years it has been covered in sand.

Practising paragraphs.

Nelson Handwriting Resources and Assessment Book 3 and Book 4 © Anita Warwick, Nelson Thornes Ltd, 2003

unit 8

Extension Resource

Book 4

Nelson

Handwriting

Name _____ Date _____

Read this passage. Divide the passage into two paragraphs, each about a different main idea. Write the two paragraphs. Remember to indent the first word of each paragraph.

> Many stone temples were built on Malta between 3600 BC and 2500 BC. The oldest have walls at least 6m long and 3.5m tall. The most impressive temple is the Hypogeum, carved on three levels deep underground. Later, wood or stone circles called henges, such as Stonehenge in England, were built. Stonehenge was built over many centuries from about 2800 BC to 1400 BC. The first Stonehenge was a circular earthwork made up of a bank and ditch. Later, large blocks of shaped stones were put up.

Practising paragraphs.

Nelson Handwriting Resources and Assessment Book 3 and Book 4 © Anita Warwick, Nelson Thornes Ltd, 2003

disbelief	*disappointed*	*dishearten*
disagreed	*disguise*	*distracted*

A   Complete each sentence with the correct word from above.

1 Gemma stared in _____ as she watched the alien spaceship land.

2 She shouted for everyone to come and see but they were _____ by the television.

3 Gemma felt _____ when no one would believe her.

4 Gemma's brother said it was probably an aeroplane in _____.

5 Gemma _____ when everyone told her it must have been a dream.

B   Write the sentences on to a sheet of paper. Keep your letters in correct proportion to each other.

Practising keeping letters in the correct proportion.

Nelson Handwriting Resources and Assessment Book 3 and Book 4 © Anita Warwick, Nelson Thornes Ltd, 2003

Name _____ Date _____

Copy this poem on to plain paper. Put guidelines underneath. Remember to keep your letters in the correct proportion to each other.

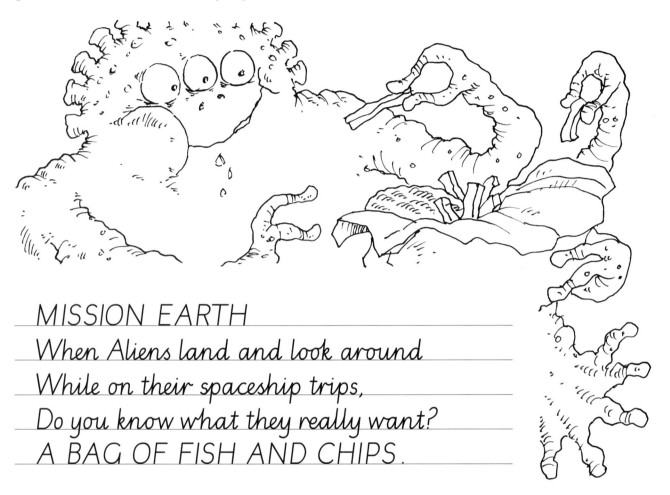

MISSION EARTH
When Aliens land and look around
While on their spaceship trips,
Do you know what they really want?
A BAG OF FISH AND CHIPS.

They might be quite advanced, it's true,
But way up there in space
They don't sell mushy peas and chips
Or haddock, cod and plaice.

And that's the reason UFOs
Never stay too long –
They find a chippy, get their chips
And then that's it – they're gone!

By *Clive Webster*

Practising keeping letters in the correct proportion.

Nelson Handwriting Resources and Assessment Book 3 and Book 4 © Anita Warwick, Nelson Thornes Ltd, 2003

Name _____ Date _____

Copy this certificate into the space below and decorate it with your own border.

> ## CERTIFICATE
>
> *Winner of the Aliens Fancy Dress Competition*
>
> Name _____
>
> *Congratulations!*
> *You have won first prize in the*
> *Aliens Fancy Dress Competition.*

Practising presentation.

Nelson Handwriting Resources and Assessment Book 3 and Book 4 © Anita Warwick, Nelson Thornes Ltd, 2003

A Copy this letter on to the notepaper below.

28 Ashley Croft
Oxford OX2 HRD
16th October 2003

Dear Stuart,
    Thank you for inviting me to your birthday party.
I had a great time. The Aliens Fancy Dress Competition
was fun, even though my hair is still purple!
    Dad says you can stay next weekend. Can you come?
Best wishes from
    Andrew

B Now write a reply on a sheet of paper. Remember the address and the date.

Practising presentation.

Nelson Handwriting Resources and Assessment Book 3 and Book 4 © Anita Warwick, Nelson Thornes Ltd, 2003

unit 11

Focus Resource

Book 4

Nelson
Handwriting

Name _____ Date _____

because   Therefore   However

so   but   even though

A Choose one of the connectives from above to fill in each gap.

1 Always keep fireworks in a box _____ make sure the lid is kept shut.

2 Matches can burn your fingers _____ use a taper to light fireworks.

3 A spark could set a firework alight. _____ never put fireworks in your pocket.

4 Never return to a firework once it has been lit _____ you think it is not alight.

5 Never throw fireworks _____ someone could get badly burnt.

6 Fireworks should be lit by an adult. _____, children can watch from a safe distance.

B Write the sentences neatly and carefully on to a sheet of paper.

Practising writing instructions.

Extension Resource

Book 4

Name _____ Date _____

A Follow these instructions to help you design and make your own poster.

1 Make a rough draft of what you want to write and draw on your poster.

2 If you want a border, draw a margin in faint pencil all the way round your paper.

3 Decide how many lines of writing you want to fit on the page.

4 Using a ruler and pencil, draw three faint lines for each line of writing. These lines will help to make all your letters the correct height and size.

5 You need to centre each line of your text. Allow 4mm for each letter and 4mm for each space between the letters. For each line, count the letters in your text and add the number of spaces. Then multiply by 4.

6 Measure the width of the page in mm. Take away the space needed for the text (in 5 above) and then divide by 2. This is the distance from the left of the page, where you start to write. This is only a rough guide but it will help you centre your writing and make it look attractive.

7 Have a go! You may need several attempts to get the design the way you want it to look.

8 When you have finished, rub out all the pencil lines.

Firework Display

Roundwood Park
Sunday 3rd November 2002
7.30 p.m.
Admission £3.00

B Now write some instructions on how to design and make a birthday card. Remember to number them.

Practising writing instructions.

Focus Resource

unit 12

Book 4

Nelson
Handwriting

Name _____ Date _____

A These instructions for making pizza have been written in the wrong order.
Read the instructions. Write in numbers to indicate the correct order.

How to Make Pizza

___ Add chopped tomatoes and cheese and bake in a hot oven.

___ Rub 100g margarine into the flour and salt until it resembles fine breadcrumbs.

___ Turn out the soft dough and knead until smooth.

___ Sift 450g self-raising flour and 1 tsp salt into a bowl.

___ Roll out the dough into a circular shape.

___ Add 300ml milk to the breadcrumb mixture and mix to a soft dough.

B Write the instructions in the correct sequence on a sheet of paper.

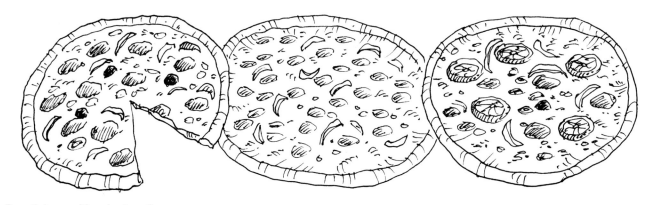

Practising writing instructions.

Nelson Handwriting Resources and Assessment Book 3 and Book 4 © Anita Warwick, Nelson Thornes Ltd, 2003

Name _____ Date _____

Use these rules about wearing seat belts to make a safety poster on plain paper.
Think of a heading and use bullet points to separate the instructions. Decide whether
to use the print alphabet. Add a decorative border.

- You MUST wear a seat belt if one is available, unless you are exempt.

- You should wear seat belts in large minibuses and coaches where available.

- The driver MUST ensure that all children under 14 years of age wear seat belts or sit in an approved child restraint.

- The driver must ensure that children do not sit behind the rear seats in an estate car or hatchback, unless a special child seat has been fitted.

- The driver must make sure that a rear-facing baby seat is NEVER fitted into a seat protected by an airbag.

Practising writing instructions.

Nelson Handwriting Resources and Assessment Book 3 and Book 4 © Anita Warwick, Nelson Thornes Ltd, 2003

Children in a class did a project about the first moon landing. They made this chart to show the rocket launches that led up to it.

Date	Spacecraft
February 1962	Mercury
March 1965	Voskhod 2
April 1961	Vostok 1
December 1968	Apollo 8
July 1969	Apollo 11
August 1962	Vostok 3 and 4
May 1961	Mercury
August 1961	Vostok 2
June 1965	Gemini 4
June 1963	Vostok 6

Fill in this blank chart with the events from above in date order. The first one is done to help you.

April 1961	

Practising presenting a project.

Nelson Handwriting Resources and Assessment Book 3 and Book 4 © Anita Warwick, Nelson Thornes Ltd, 2003

Name _____ Date _____

These verses are about how it might feel to land on the moon. Copy them neatly on to a sheet of paper. Draw a border to suit the verses.

ASTRONAUTS AND CROSSES

I lay down by the Sea of Tranquillity
And drew pictures in the dust –
A house with a chimney, two windows, a door,
A path, some flowers, a tree.
I have had some time now to adjust.
I won't see my world any more,
Except from a distance, like a misty beacon.

I imagined a game of lunar football:
A visored striker ghosting through
Defenders, in slow motion, to shoot
The golden goal to beat them all,
Like a fiery comet swerving through the blue.
Spectators in their spacesuits might be mute,
But the scorer would be over the moon.

By *Paul Sidley*

Practising presenting a project.

Nelson Handwriting Resources and Assessment Book 3 and Book 4 © Anita Warwick, Nelson Thornes Ltd, 2003

Focus Resource   **Book 4**

Nelson

Handwriting

Name _____ Date _____

Copy this passage. Remember to join your letters at or near the top, to slope your writing slightly to the right and to write fluently and legibly.

Over a period of 2,000 years, the Ancient Greeks laid many of the foundations of the modern world. Some of their ideas about medicine, mathematics, and government are still in use today. They also introduced theatre, new ways in art, and building styles that can still be seen around us. Theirs was a civilisation of spectacular achievements as they travelled, traded and fought their way through the known world.

Practising fluency.

Nelson Handwriting Resources and Assessment Book 3 and Book 4 © Anita Warwick, Nelson Thornes Ltd, 2003

Name _____ Date _____

A Copy this Ancient Greek legend about Medusa on to a sheet of paper.
Use neat, fluent handwriting. Remember to slope your writing slightly
to the right and to join your letters correctly.

Medusa was one of three monsters called the Gorgons.
They had the bodies of women, snakes for hair, teeth like
the tusks of wild boars, sharp claws and wings of gold.
Anyone who dared to look at the face of a Gorgon was
turned to stone in horror.

The young hero Perseus was on a quest to kill Medusa.
Fortunately, he had the help of the gods. Athena, the
goddess of war, went with him on his journey. Hermes,
messenger of the gods, gave him a sharp knife to cut off
her head. Some nymphs gave him a pair of winged
sandals so that he could fly, a magic helmet to make
him invisible, and a special pouch to keep Medusa's
head in if he was successful.

One final gift was from Athena herself. She handed
Perseus a shield. "It contains no magic, but it is vital to
your task," she explained.

"It's beautiful," said Perseus, admiring the gleaming
shield. The bronze was so highly polished that he could
see his face in it.

"Use it as a mirror," said the goddess, and the young
hero understood.

From *'Ancient Greek Myths and Legends'* by *Philip Ardagh*

B Underline the pronouns. The first few are done to help you.

Practising fluency.

Nelson Handwriting Resources and Assessment Book 3 and Book 4 © Anita Warwick, Nelson Thornes Ltd, 2003

possibly allow carry difficult different
annoy offer possess accident marvellous
feel look sunny little necessary

Choose a word from above that has a similar meaning to each word in this list.
Write the words next to each other. The first one is done to help you.

perhaps	perhaps	possibly
permit		
touch		
astonishing		
hold		
own		
gaze		
mishap		
essential		
small		
bright		
vex		
hard		
unusual		
bargain		

Practising writing double letters.

Nelson Handwriting Resources and Assessment Book 3 and Book 4 © Anita Warwick, Nelson Thornes Ltd, 2003

Name _____ Date _____

A Copy this poem on to a sheet of paper. Make sure your letters are the correct height and size.

BURIED TREASURE
In the heart of the forest
Where feet rarely tread,
A treasure lies buried
In a soft earthy bed.

No jewels of a princess,
No coins of gold;
No silver once hoarded
By pirates of old.

What is this treasure?
One day we may see;
Till then it lies hidden –
The seed of a tree!

by *Ronald Kay*

B Underline the words in the poem that contain double letters, such as f<u>ee</u>t.

Practising writing double letters.

Nelson Handwriting Resources and Assessment Book 3 and Book 4 © Anita Warwick, Nelson Thornes Ltd, 2003

Name _____ Date _____

A Practise writing these patterns on plain paper. Gradually increase your speed.

VVVVVV   vvvvvvv   VVVVV

ccccccccc   ccccccccc   ccccccccc

B Copy this sentence. Try to improve the smoothness of your writing as well as the speed.

Writing quickly helps me keep up with the teacher!

C Copy this sentence. Remember to move your hand at a steady speed with no jerky movements.

No matter how fast I write I must keep my writing steady!

D Find your writing speed. Divide the number of letters written by the number of minutes taken, like this:

$$\frac{\text{Number of letters written}}{\text{Number of minutes taken}} = \text{writing speed (in letters per minute)}$$

Record your score here.

My writing speed is ⬚ letters per minute.

Practising speedwriting.

Name _____ Date _____

A Practise writing these patterns until you can write them quickly, evenly and smoothly. Use plain paper.

vvvvvvvvvvvvvv   vvvvvvvvvvvv

ooooooooooooo   ooooooooooooo

eeeeeeeeeeeeee   eeeeeeeeeeeeee

wwwwwwwwwww   wwwwwwwwwww

amamamama   wewewewewew

B This is a list of 20 words to do with treasure. Copy the words quickly but legibly.

box	cash
chest	coins
fortune	funds
gems	gold
hidden	jewels
jewellery	money
necklaces	notes
pearls	riches
rings	silver
valuables	wealth

Practising speedwriting.

Nelson Handwriting Resources and Assessment Book 3 and Book 4 © Anita Warwick, Nelson Thornes Ltd, 2003

Name _____ Date _____

lion	bee	snail	mouse
owl	ice	rake	peacock

Choose the correct word from above to complete each simile.
Copy the completed similes neatly.

as slow as a _____

as thin as a _____

as wise as an _____

as proud as a _____

as busy as a _____

as cold as _____

as brave as a _____

as quiet as a _____

Ensuring letters are in the correct proportion.

Name _____ Date _____

A Copy these six similes neatly.

as cunning as a fox   _as brown as a berry_

as gentle as a lamb   _as quick as lightning_

as poor as a church mouse   _as easy as winking_

B Complete each of these sentences with a simile from above.

1 The beggar had no food and no money.
He was

2 I have never seen anyone move so fast.
She was

3 Sam is always playing clever tricks.
She is

4 The farmer works out in the sun all day.
He is

5 The sums we had to do were really simple.
They were

6 The nurse was very careful with my broken arm.
She was

Ensuring letters are in the correct proportion.

Nelson Handwriting Resources and Assessment Book 3 and Book 4 © Anita Warwick, Nelson Thornes Ltd, 2003

Name _____ Date _____

A ▶ Write the lines of this acrostic poem in the correct order.
The poem is called CATS.

Trying to catch mice,

Creeping about softly,

Scampering and squeaking.

Awake at night,

_____

_____

_____

_____

B ▶ Now write the poem neatly in the box below. Make it look as attractive as you can. Add a border.

Practising presentation.

Nelson Handwriting Resources and Assessment Book 3 and Book 4 © Anita Warwick, Nelson Thornes Ltd, 2003

Extension Resource   Book 4

Nelson Handwriting

Name _____ Date _____

Copy this poem on to plain paper. Make it look as attractive as you can.
Illustrate the poem with a picture or a border.

CATALOG

Cats sleep fat and walk thin.
Cats, when they sleep, slump;
When they wake, pull in –
And where the plump's been
There's skin.
Cats walk thin.

Cats wait in a lump,
Jump in a streak.
Cats, when they jump, are sleek
As a grape slipping its skin –
They have technique.
Oh, cats don't creak,
They sneak.

By *Rosalie Moore*

Practising presentation.

Nelson Handwriting Resources and Assessment Book 3 and Book 4 © Anita Warwick, Nelson Thornes Ltd, 2003

Name _____ Date _____

A This fact sheet is for a theme park called Dreadnought Land.
Copy the fact sheet. Remember to use print letters.

DREADNOUGHT LAND
Grapple with the Titans on the Mountains of Mars!
Track the Giant Jellyfish through the
Fifty-Fathom Falls!

B Present this information about Wonderland as a fact sheet. Use print letters.

You can visit the <u>Last Chance Saloon</u> to meet Dead-Eye Dick and his friends.
In the <u>Spooky Castle</u> you will meet many unexpected new friends, or you can
take an exciting trip down the <u>Ride the Rapids River</u>.

WONDERLAND

Practising printing.

Nelson Handwriting Resources and Assessment Book 3 and Book 4 © Anita Warwick, Nelson Thornes Ltd, 2003

Name _____ Date _____

This chart shows the prices in pounds of two-day breaks at Dreadnought Land in different hotels in different months.

		JUNE				JULY AND AUGUST			
		BY TRAIN		BY PLANE		BY TRAIN		BY PLANE	
		Adult	Child	Adult	Child	Adult	Child	Adult	Child
HOTEL A	£	286	121	304	160	346	132	337	157
HOTEL B	£	327	124	336	162	408	133	394	158
HOTEL C	£	434	125	447	163	539	134	528	159

A Copy the chart. Remember to use print letters.

B Complete this sentence. Then copy the sentence neatly.

The cheapest two-day break for two adults and two children is by train to Hotel A in June. This costs £_____.

Practising printing.

Nelson Handwriting Resources and Assessment Book 3 and Book 4 © Anita Warwick, Nelson Thornes Ltd, 2003

Focus Resource

unit 20

Book 4

Nelson

Handwriting

Name _____ Date _____

Some people develop their handwriting style by adding loops to **f**, **g**, **j** and **y** and joining **b**, **p** and **q**, like this:

f   g   j   y   b   p   q

Copy this poem. Make a join after **b** and **p** and a loop from **f**, **g**, and **j**.

LOST
In a terrible fog I once lost my way,
Where I had wandered I could not say,
I found a signpost just by a fence,
But I could not read it, the fog was so dense.
Slowly but surely, frightened to roam,
I climbed up the post for my nearest way home,
Striking a match, I turned cold and faint,
These were the words on it: 'Mind the wet paint'.

By *James Godden*

Developing an individual handwriting style.

Name _____ Date _____

A Copy these lines on to a sheet of paper in your usual handwriting style.

Over the Channel now, beneath the enchanting
Inane babble of a baby-blue sky,
We soar through cloudland, at the height of nonsense,
From a distance they might be sifted sugar drifts,
Meringues, iced cakes, confections of whipped cream
Lavishly piled for some Olympian party –
A child's idea of heaven.

From *'Flight to Italy'* by C. Day Lewis

Some people develop their writing with loops and joins from **b** and **p**, like this:

Over the Channel now, beneath the enchanting
Inane babble of a baby-blue sky,
We soar through cloudland, at the height of nonsense,
From a distance they might be sifted sugar drifts,
Meringues, iced cakes, confections of whipped cream
Lavishly piled for some Olympian party-
A child's idea of heaven.

B Write the lines with loops and with joins from **b** and **p** on to a sheet of paper.

Developing an individual handwriting style.